The Temple of Isis on the island of
Philae, drawing by F. Catherwood.

F. CATHERWOOD, ARCHITECT-EXPLORER OF TWO WORLDS

F. Catherwood

ARCHITECT-EXPLORER *of* TWO WORLDS

by VICTOR WOLFGANG von HAGEN

with an introduction by ALDOUS HUXLEY

BARRE PUBLISHERS

Barre, Massachusetts 1968

Yum Kax, Lord of Harvest, Copan. Engraved
for Incidents of Travel in Central America.

Copyright © 1967 by Victor Wolfgang von Hagen
Library of Congress Catalog Card Number 67-25571
Barre Publishers, Barre, Massachusetts
Design: Frank Lieberman
Composed and Printed in the United States of America

678-401

CONTENTS

INTRODUCTION *by* ALDOUS HUXLEY

*I*T WAS IN Guatemala, while trying to do a little sketching among the most unbelievably picturesque ruins of Antigua, that I first became interested in Frederick Catherwood. With his drawings of Mayan steles and temples — or rather with the woodcuts, which other hands than his had made, none too competently, after those drawings — I was, of course, already familiar. But to the man who was responsible for those amazingly accurate and vivid works of documentary art, I had previously given no thought. My concern with Catherwood as a person was aroused by the insects. To the would-be landscape painter, even in salubrious Antigua, these are a very severe trial. I bore with them for a couple of hours, then packed up my paints, discomfited and full of a new admiration for the man who had made the illustrations to Stephens's *Incidents of Travel*. From dawn till dusk, day after day and for weeks at a stretch, this martyr to archaeology had exposed himself to all the winged and crawling malice of tropical nature. Ticks, ants, wasps, flies, mosquitoes; they had bitten him, stung him, drunk his blood, infected him with malaria. But the man had grimly gone on drawing. Itching, swollen, burning or shuddering with fever, he had filled whole portfolios with the measured plans and elevations of temples, with studies of Mayan sculpture so scientifically accurate that modern experts in pre-Columbian history can spell out the date of a stele from Catherwood's representations of its, to him, incomprehensible hieroglyphs.

This gifted artist, this conscientiously precise and careful observer, this indomitable Prometheus, self-chained to his camp-stool while mosquitoes brought him again and again to the very gates of death — who was he? Returning from Central America to libraries and books of reference, I tried to find out — but with absolutely no success. Catherwood remained merely a name and nothing more. But now Mr. Victor von Hagen, an explorer of jungles who is also an explorer of explorers, has undertaken the task of restoring to this name a history and a personality. Thanks to his labors we now know where Catherwood was born, how he was educated, to what temples, pyramids, mosques, and acropolises his passion for archaeology took him. And we know, too, that Catherwood was dogged throughout his whole career as an archaeologist and artist by a bad luck, so perfectly adapted to thwart his ambitions, so exquisitely designed to frustrate all his best efforts, as to seem the conscious working of a kind of negative Providence. Most of his innumerable studies of Egyptian ruins remained unpublished, and the same fate was reserved for his elaborate architectural drawings — the first ever made — of the Mosque of Omar at Jerusalem. Later, when he began to make money in New York, his crowd-drawing panorama of the Holy City was destroyed by fire, and along with the circular building and his enormous painting, hundreds of original drawings brought back from Central America were also destroyed. After that, it is not surprising to learn, Catherwood abandoned the unequal struggle with a Destiny, which evidently had no intention of allowing him to be a successful artist and archaeologist. He packed up, parked a wife and perhaps a child or two, and vanished.

What's become of Waring,
Since he gave us all the slip?

Alas, it was not in Vishnu-land that this precursor of Browning's hero was to be found; it was not over the Kremlin's pavement that he "stepped with five other generals, who simultaneously take snuff"; it was not even to the romantic obscurity of a Triestine bumboat that he had retired. Poor Catherwood had disappeared into British Guiana, where, no longer calling himself an architect or painter or archaeologist, but a civil engineer, he was building

x

the first railway to be laid down on the soil of South America. Or, to be more precise, he was trying to build it. Good artists, as Rimbaud was to demonstrate a generation later, are rarely good businessmen or administrators. Besides, this particular project turned out to be unexpectedly difficult. The terrain was marshy; the Negro laborers would not labor; the white planters were unsympathetic; the climate and the insects were, if possible, worse than those of Yucatán and Guatemala. Catherwood's negative Providence was still busily at work upon him. After a year or two he threw in the sponge and retired, by way of Panama, to newly booming California. Here, it seems, he might at long last have prospered. But this was something which his Destiny could obviously not permit. It put into his head the idea of paying a visit to England and, on the return voyage, arranged a collision on the high seas, which sent the one-time artist and archaeologist, along with many other passengers, to the bottom of the Atlantic.

Thus ended Frederick Catherwood, plunging irretrievably and forever into that ocean of oblivion, from which, even in life, he had hardly succeeded in emerging. For not only had he failed to receive that public recognition to which his talents entitled him; he seems also, in some sort, to have missed even private recognition. He was the friend and collaborator of painters and draftsmen; yet no likeness of him was ever made — or, at any rate, none is now extant. He worked for many months with a vivid and copious writer, and he had met, in the course of his wandering life, many journalists in search of copy and many archaeologists who shared his special interests; and yet none of them has left us an account of his personality or of the details of his private life. In spite of Mr. von Hagen's researches, the man whose strange and in many ways tragic career he has now reconstructed remains profoundly mysterious. We know what he did; but we still have very little idea what he was like, or how he thought or felt.

Professionally speaking, Catherwood belongs to a species — the artist-archaeologist — which is all but extinct. What the rifle did to *Bos bison,* the camera has done to that breed of which Piranesi was the most celebrated specimen and Catherwood his not unworthy successor. In the fiftieth of a second a man with a Leica can do what Catherwood could accomplish only at the cost of long, agonizing days among the insects, followed by months or years of intermittent fever. Or, to be more accurate, the man with the Leica can do *some* of the things that Catherwood and Piranesi did, and do them better than even the most masterly and conscientious of draftsmen. But when we pass from the precise reproduction of architectural and sculptural details to the rendering of great monuments in their totality, as their creators meant them to be seen and as the mind behind the spectator's eyes actually perceives them, the advantage is not always with the photographer. The camera is unable, while it does its recordings, to turn its head or lift its eyes. Except from a great distance, it cannot take in the whole of a large monument, while at close range it sees receding lines and surfaces in a perspective that, by human standards, always seems exaggerated. No photograph of the Colosseum or the aqueducts of the Campagna, of Castel Sant'-Angelo or the Roman basilicas can compare (leaving out of account all questions of intrinsic beauty) even in mere truthfulness with the etchings of Piranesi. For Piranesi renders not only the details but also the impression made by the monuments as artistic wholes.

It is only by taking many partial views that the photographer is able to make up for his instrument's inability to render the full effect of architectural totality. And, of course, this endless capacity for partial views does in fact make the camera more useful to the archaeologist than the pencil, even though, given a sufficiency of time, talent and resistance to insects, he can do things with the pencil which are beyond the scope of his optical machine. But time is limited, talent is rare, and mosquitoes distressingly abundant. Hence the extinction of the proud race or artist-archaeologists. Catherwood and his kind have now gone the way of engravers on steel and copper, of the mezzotinters, the woodblock makers, and those wonderful cartoonist-lithographers and journalist-draftsmen, of whom Daumier and Constantin Guys were the greatest. Illustrated papers now rely on snapshots and process blocks, and pictures are reproduced by collotype or photogravure. The second-rate artists, who were once so usefully employed in making intrinsically beautiful reproductions of the works of their betters, are now at liberty to devote the whole of their attention to "creative work." In other words, they are now free to spend all their time producing the rubbish, of which alone, as original artists, they are capable.

Aldous Huxley

WHO was Catherwood?

The name is uncommon enough; yet anyone who has had interest in the Mayas will recognize it instantly: Frederick Catherwood, collaborator and friend of John Lloyd Stephens, was illustrator of the books that first revealed the wonders of the Maya civilization to the modern world.

Yet this Catherwood was much else; he was a pioneer in Egyptology, having spent the greater part of his years — between 1824-32 — up and down and around the Nile; he was the first to limn the Saracenic architecture. He traveled widely in the classical lands. The co-discoverer of the Maya civilization, was also an architect who raised monuments and mansions in New York, a surveyor who built the first railroad in South America; he was archaeologist, traveler, engineer, panoramist, all this and all this in vain: the mechanics of oblivion engulfed Catherwood dead as well as alive.

None of his well-placed friends in the half century of his life ever wrote a word-description of him; no one sketched him and although he was the first to use a daguerreotype to photograph Maya ruins he never sat for his own self-portrait — or if he did, this, like so much else of him, has disappeared in the stream of time.

Catherwood appears only as a shadowy and indistinct figure moving against a sharply detailed background of persons and places. When he finally gave up his unequal struggle with this all-hating world and lost in a disaster at sea and even in death a certain primacy (he died in the first collision in history of steam-driven ships) — he sank not only out of his contemporaries' sight but as well out of human memory. Until I published my first biography of him, in 1950, libraries merely wrote his name in their catalogues as "F. Catherwood (?)" as though his very existence was doubted; he appeared, it hardly need be said, in only one biographical dictionary. So that to unearth the most rudimentary facts about him has been less a problem of scholarship than one of archaeology; a restoration had to be made out of the broken and scattered potsherds of his life.

Frederick Catherwood's Egyptian drawings lie entombed in the huge folios of the Robert Hay collections in the British Museum, unpublished until they first appeared in my book in 1950. His minute scale drawings of the Dome of the Rock have disappeared without trace; his architectural studies of ancient monuments throughout the Middle East and North Africa — lost. His many panoramas of ruined cities have been destroyed by fires and holocausts. There remains for a valuation, then, his own work on the Mayas — and even that which survives is only a fraction of what he drew. There can be no appeal to impartial posterity. Time has lost three quarters of the written works of antiquity. Varius, we are told, was equal to Virgil; he has perished without a trace. Aelian was a fool: he survives. Even in the ages of advanced culture, posterial recognition of talent is not just. There are no fixed rules. And none will fit our Mr. Catherwood.

However, it is abundantly clear the influence he had on Stephens's judgement as regards the origin and age of the Maya structural monuments. Catherwood brought to the first days of American archaeology fifteen years of experience from the Old World. In a century when antiquarians held passionately to the idea that the ruins found in Mexico and Central America were the work of either Egyptians, Greeks, Carthaginians, or some wayward Semitic tribes, Catherwood, contrary to all else wrote: "Mr. Stephens and myself after a full and precise comparative survey of the ancient ruins . . . concluded that they [the ruins] are not of immemorial antiquity, the work of unknown races, but that as we now see them, they were occupied and ... erected by the Indian tribes in possession of the country at the time of the Spanish conquest — that they are the production of an indigenous school of art, adapted to the natural circumstances of the country and to the civil and religious policy then prevailing — and that they present but very slight and accidental analogies with the works of any people or country in the Old World."

In the seventeen years' interval since I published Catherwood's first and only biography nothing has been dredged up from the stream of time to change his life-pattern then laid down. However, details of "Catherwood" have risen to the surface. The archives of the Panama Railroad Company (in New York), the rail-line which was built by Stephens and with Catherwood's aid, disgorged a sizable amount of records, mostly letters, wills, and account books, and added further details to the Catherwood image. An unedited Diary of Joseph Bonomi, through the courtesy of Mrs. Anthony de Cosson and the Griffith Institute, Ashmolean Museum, Oxford has been used. In addition an unedited narrative of Henry Westcar — one of the "Nilitic Englishmen" of the period — which was long in the possession of the late Egyptologist Dr. L. Keimer, has come to me through the courtesy of the German Archaeological Institute in Cairo.

It is a pleasure to acknowledge the courtesies of the Trustees of the British Museum who allowed the Catherwood material to be published for the first time, and as well, the Bancroft Library of the University of California at Berkeley for permission to use the Stephens-Catherwood material in their collections.

I only hope that with these new literary gleanings Frederick Catherwood will take on added flesh to clothe his bare archaeological bones, and that now he really has more substance than old Banquo's ghost.

V. W. v. H.
Rome, MCMLXVII

XV

REDERICK CATHERWOOD began well enough. His eyes opened, in 1799, in London's Hoxton Parish during the late Georgian period of candlelight, powdered periwigs and rhymed couplets. The Catherwoods were neither well-placed nor misplaced; they were gentry with a touch of the literary and certainly some competence since the house where Frederick Catherwood was born, and that still stands in Charles Square, is a graceful building with architectural echoes of affluence and good taste.

Hoxton, in London's suburbs, was not then, as it was later to become, the "Queen of Unloveliness." It still had an air about it. Shakespeare had acted in Hoxton at the theater called The Curtain; Ben Jonson fought his duel with Gabriel Spender; Keats lived close by; Mary Wollstonecraft Godwin who wrote *Frankenstein* and lived with Shelley was a Hoxtonian; and as a boy Catherwood walked past the insane asylum, Balmes House (hence "balmy"), where Mary Lamb had been confined after she had killed her mother with a carving knife.

There is little known about the other "Catherwoods." The name, sufficiently unusual, appears occasionally in the registers; in the middle of the 18th century a John James Catherwood enters the lists. This "Catherwood" was Frederick's uncle, who resided at 21, Charles Square, Hoxton.

Immediately next door at Number 20 was the residence of the other Catherwoods; they were Nathaniel and Elizabeth, the parents of our Mr. Catherwood. He was born in that house 27 February, 1799.

North of the Thames, eight miles beyond the Old Lady of Threadneedle Street, where Bishopsgate Street becomes Hackney Road, lies the metropolitan Borough of Shoreditch. Once a village on the old Roman road, Shoreditch is composed of two districts, one of which (called "Hochestone" in the Domesday Book) is the hamlet of Hoxton. In ancient times a village, Hoxton was then a prebend of St. Paul's Cathedral, an extraparochial district, "where the inhabitants married and buried where they pleased."

Charles Square, Hoxton, where the Catherwoods lived was a small, charming square surrounded by houses built about 1770 — and, as the *Shoreditch Observer* recorded, "occupied by a highly respectable class of persons." Two of these houses facing Charles Square, houses with classical doors and iron grills, were the Catherwoods'.

While the Napoleonic wars raged in Europe, Frederick Catherwood sought an education. For young people then without family position, an education or a place in the world was not easily acquired; education for those of meager circumstances was difficult. Catherwood doubtless attended one of those homespun day schools near to Charles Square which opened facilities to the children of Hoxton. There, presumably, Catherwood remained to the Eighth Form studying Accidence and Grammar, and becoming, at least to the satisfaction of the awarded certificates, "a perfect grammarian, a good Orator and Poet, well instructed in Latin, Greek, and Hebrew." As short as it was, it must have been basically good, for Catherwood became later an excellent linguist, able to speak Arabic, Greek, and Italian, and read, if not write, Hebrew. He also had enough "Mathematicks" to prepare him for his profession.

It was outside his classes that his life interest developed: he became passionately interested in architecture.

Catherwood wandered with his friend, Joseph Bonomi, through the labyrinths of London's alleys and lanes, where new buildings were rising to ornament England's Augustan Age. Severn, also Hoxton-born although four years the senior of Catherwood, who would enter literary history as the friend of John Keats, was already apprenticed to William Bond, the engraver, of Newman Street, Hoxton. Presumably Severn's decision gave Catherwood the needed inspiration, for when he reached sixteen he left school and went to Michael Meredith, the architect, who lived on Bishopsgate Road. In 1815 Catherwood signed articles of apprenticeship.

TWO

The ROMANTIC AGONY

FREDERICK CATHERWOOD, accompanying his master, Michael Meredith, Archt., made a topographical tour of England. It was the day of the beautifully illustrated architectural book made popular by John Britton, and Meredith followed this trend, dragging his apprentice with him. Nothing much is known of Michael Meredith except for his exhibition record at the Royal Academy. Under Meredith, Catherwood learned his craft. He was taught the mechanics of drawing, isometrical projection, perspective, and skiagraphy, and under Meredith's tutorship he became an excellent performer with T-square and compass. Between the intervals of work Catherwood cleaned the palettes, sketched in the rough work of his master, and did the thousand and one disagreeable tasks of an apprentice. For five years he lived on a pittance and learned his profession.

There were limitations to his apprenticeship with Michael Meredith. Catherwood found after five years that he had gone as far as he could with this master. In 1820 he received back his apprentice-indentures and immediately began to work on his first exhibition piece.

Curiously enough, no one has ever described Catherwood, and his own self-portrait is but a luminous blur. Although he was known personally to almost every important artist or architect of his time and to many of the artists studying in Rome and to the regiment of artist-explorers (his colleagues) who toured Egypt (and although later he was a personal friend of most of the National Academicians in New York City), no one, for unfathomable reasons, ever drew or painted the reticent "Mr. Catherwood" — at least there is no known record of any portrait of him. Even among the hundred drawings of William Brockedon — now in the British Museum — containing pencilings of almost every one of Catherwood's contemporaries, there is none of him. In a rare autobiographical gesture Catherwood made a self-portrait of himself and his friend Joseph Bonomi for a "Panorama of Jerusalem," but this has been destroyed. There remains only his other self-portrait, in miniature and unclear, standing before one of the ruins of the Mayan site of Tulum. He is here pictured as a mature man of forty-two, he drew himself as he undoubtedly was — as ruggedly constructed as a Dorchester fishing-boat. Here he is pictured light-haired and blue-eyed. One can make out no more. Nor is there a word description of Catherwood; he is only referred to, even by his most intimate friends, as "Mr. Catherwood." John Lloyd Stephens, who knew him intimately for fifteen years, and traveled with him through strife-torn Central America, enduring with him imprisonment, disease, and incredible hardships, speaks of him only in this manner.

Catherwood, himself, is responsible for the meagerness of his personal history; there was some fundamental disequilibrium in his psyche. He was modest to a fault; he pushed the classic English virtues — dignity, serenity, reticence — to such a point that he diminished his own personality. Formal and restrained, he exhibited early symptoms of melancholia. Yet he had enthusiasm, despite his reserved and retiring manner, and this was to sustain him while, in the narrow corners of some lost world, he delineated the remains of forgotten civilizations.

In 1820, under Joseph Severn's guidance, Catherwood began to attend the free art classes of the Royal Academy in London. Held at Somerset House, the school was open to qualified pupils.

Sir John Soane gave the lectures on architecture. Although given in his small colorless voice, still his lectures were the popular feature of the Royal Academy. In attendance were many young architectural students with whom Catherwood would make archaeological history — T. J. Donaldson, Henry Parke, Francis Arundale, Joseph John Scoles, and Joseph Bonomi.

Soane, "the most original British architect since Vanbrugh," was a twinkle-eyed enthusiastic little man. The son of a bricklayer, he had been articled out to the architect George Dance. Later he studied at the Royal Academy and, in the year that the American colonies were declaring themselves independent, he won the society's Gold Medal. He traveled in Italy and Greece, and in Rome he "discovered" Piranesi.

It was in Soane's classes that Catherwood was introduced to Piranesi. It was a feverish moment when Soane exhibited the huge volume of Piranesi's *Della magnificenza ed architettura di Roma* to his students. Catherwood, for one, was deeply moved by the manner in which Piranesi rendered the Roman ruins. It was Piranesi's treatment, his manner of conveying the impression of the great scale and magnificence of the buildings of ancient Rome that were astounding. For archaeology had early enmeshed Piranesi. After visiting Naples and Paestum he returned to Rome in 1740, where he spent the remainder of his life, "quareling with antiquarians and noble lords," but incessantly working and building for himself, by his skill as a draftsman and engraver, that monument *aere perennius,* which had been the admitted ambition of his life. Catherwood was influenced by Piranesi as by no other, and although he knew that the "art of Piranesi is not a manner to be learnt," he tried to capture in his own archaeological drawings the same intense emotion of that master.

It was directly after Catherwood had exhibited his first drawing at the Royal Academy that his future itinerary developed, one that would determine his whole career; strangely enough, it came out of the circumstance of the illness of John Keats.

Keats, in the last stages of consumption, went to Rome, for, it was hoped, the regaining of his health. Joseph Severn elected to accompany him. Severn's funds consisted only of the pittance allowed him by the Royal Academy for a year's study in Rome, and Keats's of a small advance paid by John Taylor, his publisher, againt royalties of his future poems.

In response to the fervent entreaties of Severn, morose and melancholy after Keats's death, Frederick Catherwood went to Rome. This is recorded; Joseph Severn, writing to his sister Maria on 15 September 1821, told of Catherwood's arrival at Severn's rooms at Via di San Isidoro 43 in Rome. . .

> . . . Mr. Catherwood arrived here last night in perfect health and safety after a most favourable journey. I found him sitting in my Study with the same look and manner that I recollect in London — for he is the first Friend I have met here whom I knew there — his voice and face carried me to my dear home — it is a great pleasure and will be also a mutual improvement. We have this Morg. seen St. Peters — and the Vatican — with which he is quite delighted or I should say astonished — I have introduced him to many brother Artists here — Englishmen — there are three architects among them [T. J. Donaldson, Joseph Bonomi and J. J. Scoles] — whom he will begin to study with. . . . Mr. Catherwood found me in good health and spirits — and in the midst of many delightful Studies and speculations &c with many friends — The air in Rome is not unhealthy this season — so that I have remained here at the present time the weather and air is most delicious. Mr. C[atherwood] found this in the Morg. walk — he seems most gratified with what we tell of Rome and living in it. I think he has done wisely in coming whilst he is young — he will lay a foundation here that may direct nobly all through Life. . . Mr. Catherwood begs you to show my letter at Charles Square [the residence of the Catherwoods] and prays them to excuse him writing this Post — his head is so full of Rome and Sleep and he is so tired. . .

Catherwood was welcomed into the Society of Englishmen, "all good fellows — twenty in number — Painters, Sculptors & Architects," wrote Joseph Severn. And it was in that group he began his study of classical architecture. The group was exceedingly lively and enthusiastic. One of the four architects, Thomas Leverton Donaldson, the founder-to-be of the Royal Institute of British Architects and a lifelong friend of Catherwood, had been born in Bloomsbury Square in 1795, had studied at the Royal Academy, and had been awarded its Silver Medal. Thereafter, in pursuit of the *antique,* he left for Rome.

Two other architects of the "Society of Englishmen," Scoles and Bonomi, arrived in Rome a few months after Frederick Catherwood. Scoles, the least remembered of them, had also studied the *antique* in the Royal Academy after he had finished his apprenticeship to John Ireland, architect. Born into the Catholic Church in 1798, Scoles is remembered now, if he is at all, as one of those present at Shelley's funeral; also for his great fiasco, the collapse of the suspension bridge, which he built in 1845, over the river Bure at Great Yarmouth. Scoles was a constant companion of Catherwood in the Mediterranean, and long after he married and fathered four sons and eight daughters, he remained in touch with him. It is to Joseph John Scoles that we owe the only published biographical material — tantalizing though it is — of Catherwood.

Joseph Bonomi, the famous curator of Sir John Soane's Museum at Lincoln's Inn Field, is by far the best remembered of all these members of the Society of Englishmen. As the illustrator of Sir John Gardner Wilkinson's works on Egyptian archaeology, Bonomi's name is most enduringly linked to Egypt. He was a gay small man and remembered in that circle of temperamental artists for his easy good nature. The son of Bonomi the elder (the Italian architect who had been brought from Rome on the invitation of the Brothers Adam), Joseph Bonomi was born in 1796 and inherited his father's talents. In company with Scoles he went to Rome. Later, he and Bonomi and Catherwood were included as architectural artists on the famous Egyptian expeditions of Robert Hay.

Rome, in 1822, was filled with English aristocracy who were living elegantly in the villas of impecunious Roman nobles. In that properly regal setting, the great milords made obeisance to the Muses. At that time, everyone of consequence, it seemed, was in Rome; an endless succession of artists, sculptors, architects, and writers were working in Rome under the munificence of the aristocracy, a society "which was literary, athletic, dissipated and political."

Catherwood soon found himself part of this dazzling group to which Joseph Severn had provided the key; he soon was admitted to the *conversazioni* of Roman society; "company numerous but very ill-sorted." As Henry Fox complains, "people of all descriptions without any connection or acquaintance with each other. . . gathered together and huddled up at the dinner table. . . ," combinations that included Lady Blessington, Elizabeth, the Duchess of Devonshire, Louis Bonaparte and his empty, foolish brother Jérôme, Canova, Thorwaldsen, Duc de Laval, the ephebic Count D'Orsay, Gibbon, Severn, Eastlake, Lady Westmoreland, Manuel de Godoy, the fallen Spanish prime minister, Sir William Drummond, and Edward Cheney. Such company was heady wine for young Catherwood, born of modest circumstances and of a family who prided themselves on their liberal ideas.

Catherwood also worked. For a while he was with the Duchess of Devonshire while she was directing her private excavations in the Forum; later accompanied by Henry Parke, he made his first archaeological drawings depicting the Catacombs, published in the *Dictionary of Architecture*. Then, moving southward with drafting board and easel, he went to Sicily.

In the land of Demeter, Catherwood had his first glimpse of the remains of the Greeks. He followed the eastern shore, all along the way making sketches of the ruins in the effusive and melodious style of the Romantics. He came to the ruins of Taormina, lying midway between Syracuse and Messina. All that visibly remained of Taormina was the ruins of a Greek theater excavated twenty-three centuries ago out of the living rock from the northern face of Mount Taor, and a section of ancient walls with ruined columns facing Homer's "purple sea." The scene was stirringly picturesque. In the distance, snow-crowned Mt. Etna acted as a superb backdrop, rising 10,800 feet into the blue Sicilian sky; the fabled Mt. Etna, where the Cumean Sybil abandoned Aeneas in the kingdom of mighty Dis. It was this that Catherwood painted in tempera, "Mt. Etna from the Ruins of Tauramina."* It is a *pièce du milieu;* but a superb one. As composition and drawing and in the use of color, it shows him worthy of standing beside such famous early British watercolorists as Rooker, Cox, Cotman, and Harding. When the picture was exhibited in New York at the National Academy

---

* This picture was exhibited in 1839 at the National Academy of Design in New York and appears as Number 10 "Mount Etna from the Ruins of Tauramina." It was purchased by Mr. S. S. Swords and has remained in the family for five generations; the present owner is Mrs. Frederic G. Hoppin of New York. They have known it only as "the Catherwood."

of Design in 1839, it drew exaggerated praise from Cole, himself a master of the picturesque. And Thomas Cole remembered that picture. When he went abroad in 1841 and to Sicily, he went to Taormina and painted "Mount Aetna from Taormina" (1844) from almost the same spot that Catherwood, twenty years before him, had painted his.

After Rome, Greece was for young students the architectural Mecca; for Italy, the first to feel the pulse of archaeology, had given birth in 1733 to the Society of Dilettanti, composed of learned men — mostly Englishmen — who sponsored those superbly illustrated folios on classical architecture. Accompanied by Donaldson and Scoles, Frederick Catherwood went to Athens, arriving just about the moment that Lord Byron, volunteering for service with the Greeks, landed at Missolonghi with his retinue of twelve people, five horses, two cannons, and 50,000 Spanish pesos.

We do not know what Catherwood's itinerary was in Greece or precisely what he drew. None of his Grecian drawings have come to light. All we know with certainty is what was succinctly revealed by his friend Stephens: "Mr. Catherwood... shut up in Athens during the Greek revolution when it was besieged by the Turks, pursued his artistical studies and perforce made castings with his own hands."

CATHERWOOD arrived in Egypt 1823 at the time that "Egyptianism", inspired by the publications of the French savants who had traveled with Napoleon, was taking hold. Beyond the superb beginnings of the French, little systematic work had been done. It had been only six years since Giovanni Belzoni had broken into the vaulted tombs where he had pierced the walls and entered the labyrinths, trampling on golden-plated mummies as "thick as leaves in Vallombrosa."

In the autumn of 1824 Frederick Catherwood, in company with Henry Parke and Joseph Scoles, hired a vessel and went up the Nile. Drawing and sketching on the way, they went a thousand miles beyond the first cataract into Nubian country. There, at considerable risk of life, these young architects systematically mapped the clusters of ruins in the Upper Nile. In more than one sense Catherwood's career was cast in Egypt, for later at Alexandria he met Robert Hay, a titled young man who had not, as yet, made his first Nile journey; it was Catherwood's drawings that delighted him and raised his enthusiasm ("if that is possible," he wrote); these drawings determined his interest in Egyptology.

Robert Hay of Linplum, heir to the marquisate of Tweeddale, had thought out a most ambitious archaeological program. With a retinue of experienced artists, architects, topographical draftsmen, and antiquarians (they were not yet archaeologists), he planned to go up the Nile and investigate each ruined site, known and unknown. At each he planned to have his artists draw the murals with their inscriptions, and to have the architects make ground plans of the ruins; it was to be the greatest scientific expedition since Napoleon's. Robert Hay's expedition was composed of a company of Englishmen, many of whom in later years became famous for one reason or another. The group included: Joseph Bonomi, Francis Arundale, James Haliburton (called Burton), Charles Laver, Edward W. Lane and Wilkinson (two incipient archaeologists), G. B. Greenough, George A. Hoskins, and, to end the impressive list, Frederick Catherwood. These young men, during the years 1824-33, were to lay down the basis of Egyptian archaeology.

Catherwood had first heard of Robert Hay in London when he attended the architectural lectures at the Royal Academy. A grandson of John Hay, the First Earl of Tweeddale, he had little interest in the title he would one day inherit from his brother. Robert Hay was destined to spend most of his life in the Near East, and to marry much to the chagrin of the editor of *Burke's Peerage*, Kalitza, daughter of Alexander Psaraké, chief magistrate of Apodulo at Crete. Hay used his inheritance to good purpose; at his own expense he maintained this large expedition, which remained in the field for more than ten years. He bequeathed to the British Museum, in 1879, forty-nine folio volumes of paintings, drawings, plans and panoramas of Egyptian antiquities, a monument of archaeological research. He published one book.

The expedition began its work at Memphis, the gateway to the glory of ancient Egypt. Hay's artists drew to scale the great pyramids of Giza, those of Cheops, Chephren and Mycerinus, a work in which Catherwood, for one, was engaged for some time. After Memphis, Sakkareh; then it was Abydos; by 1832, the expedition had set up its camp in the ruins of Thebes.

It was here at the ruins of the greatest cities of the ancient world - Thebes, Karnak Luxor, and Deir el- Bahari - that Robert Hay's expeditionists devoted their greatest attention. The magnificent temples built in the time of Queen Hatshepsut in 1500 B.C. (under the architectural guidance of Senenmut) crowded the banks of the Nile. The Temple of Karnak, composed of red granite cut in quarries at Aswan, was so beautiful when completed that it brought insomnia to Hatshepsut, who said that "she could not sleep because of this temple." It had virtually the same effect upon the young English architects who pitched their tents among these superbly beautiful monuments of violently polychromed limestone.

Catherwood began work in September 1832. After careful measurements he drew first a colored plan of Thebes and then a detailed plan of the whole ruins. He then worked on a panorama of the valley showing Thebes* — a sketch that would one day be enlarged into a huge scenic panorama and displayed in London and New York. Later he drew to scale the obelisks that protruded their stone tongues above the ruins. Joseph Bonomi, who displayed great skill in rendering hieroglyphics, drew the interiors of the Theban tombs, the murals, and inscriptions from the tomb of Rekhmire. In the meanwhile Charles Laver was working on Karnak, making a rough plan of the superb capital of Amenhotep III. Robert Hay assigned Francis Arundale to make views, plans, and sections of the principal buildings of Karnak, Luxor, the temples of Medinet Habu, el-Qurna, and the surrounding region; Joseph Bonomi kept to the hieroglyphics.

Toward the end of 1832 Catherwood, in company with James Haliburton, began work on the "Colossi of Memnon." Haliburton — of the Haliburtons of Roxburghshire — had come to Egypt in 1821 with Wilkinson, at the invitation of Mehemet Ali, to make a geological survey of the Nile. There, falling under the spell of the *antique,* he soon left the employ of the Pasha and went up the Nile. He published in Cairo several bulky folios entitled *Excerpta Hieroglyphica.*

On the west bank of the Nile, between the ruined structure of

* The huge circular canvas was destroyed in a fire that consumed Catherwood's rotunda in New York. The only representation of it is a wood engraving, printed in a pamphlet which guided the viewers as they moved around the circular mural. When exhibited in New York in 1836, the critic in *The Mirror* thought that "the Panorama of Thebes is beautifully painted... one can hardly rid oneself of the idea that it is not nature that he is viewing..." *A Description of a View of Thebes,* New York, 1836.

Medinet Habu and the Ramesseum, with its feet eternally lapped by the rising Nile, stood the seventy-foot-high statue of Amenhotep III. An architectural sculpture three thousand years old, it had been fashioned out of a reddish conglomerate from the sandhills of Edfu, floated down the Nile in eight especially constructed ships. Overawed by the size and grandeur of his work, the architect-sculptor of the "Colossi" glowed with enthusiasm; "They are wonderful," he said in hieroglyphics, "for size and height, and they will last as long as heaven."

Catherwood raised a scaffold on the battered faceless sides of the statues, measured in detail these wonderful monuments of the "vocal Memnon," and drew them to scale, and then he excavated about their base and discovered that they reposed only on a stratum of sand. Catherwood's drawings, the first accurate ones ever made, had never been published lying in the anonymity of the Hay collections in the British Museum. But his drawings of the Ramesseum Court, the raised terrace and the Osiride pillars of Ramses II, had a published history; they appeared in William Finden's *Landscape Illustrations of the Bible.*

The expedition continued up the Nile, working at Hierakonpolis, Edfu, and finally Elephantine and the Isle of Philae, the beauty of which made Pierre Loti weep. There Catherwood copied the inscriptions on the intaglio walls relating to Ptolemy and Cleopatra. After weeks in the temples of Philae, Catherwood had a large portfolio of drawings, among others a watercolor that he thought was good enough to retain.*

After this the expedition ended and Catherwood was assigned to oblivion. Of the hundreds of drawings and plans that form the huge Robert Hay collections, nothing of Catherwood was published until the present author found and identified his drawings in the collections in the British Museum. The material contains 49 huge folios, so vast an amount that it would take a lifetime to interpret it. Doubtless there was much that Catherwood recorded in Egypt which is now destroyed. Many of his drawings are signed with merely "F.C," many others are unsigned, so that only the ex-

* 297 Island of Philae, First cataract of the Nile — *Moonlight;* exhibited in 1845 at the National Academy of Design, New York.

perience gained from long contact with Catherwood's style alone makes identification possible. In addititon to the Robert Hay collections of manuscripts and drawings there are on deposit the collections of James Haliburton. These 67 volumes have considerable personal material on Catherwood. The mere mass of the material is awesome.

Everyone it seemed, except Catherwood, on that expedition, published a book illustrated with his own drawings. Henry Westcar, who accompanied Catherwood, wrote "A Journal of a Tour made through Egypt, Upper & Lower Nubia" in 1823-24. George Hoskins, another member of the expedition, who accompanied Catherwood to the Oasis of Kharga east of Thebes, wrote "A Visit to the Great Oasis of the Libyan Desert" (London 1837). Catherwood is often mentioned; "a pistol with seven barrels belonging to Mr. C. was considered by all the Arabs who saw it a most formidable weapon and the fame of it was widely spread through the valley of the Nile. . . ." Robert Hay did a sumptuous "Illustration of Cairo," with lithographs by John C. Bourne (London 1840). And finally there was Arundale. An architect who had aided the famed Augustus Pugin in collecting material for his "Architectural Antiquities of Normandy," Arundale was one of the original members of the Robert Hay expedition. He was an accomplished architectural draftsman, but Francis Vyvyan Jago Arundale suffered from epilepsy, and his seizures, which would come on without notice, were one of the trials of Catherwood.

Arundale published a book in which Catherwood figures, *"Illustrations of Jerusalem and Mt. Sinai"* (London 1837). But Catherwood, who seemed to be the mechanist of his own oblivion, wrote nothing. Joseph Bonomi kept a diary, here used for the first time. Their project was an archaeological survey of the deserts east of Cairo, Sinai, and then north down the great rift through Jordan, Jerusalem, and into Lebanon.*

* The present author is planning a retrospective work on Catherwood's work in Egypt, "The Lost Egyptian Journals of Frederick Catherwood," which will be based on personal visits to all Egyptian sites mentioned and the Hay collections, British Museum, Add. MSS. 29812-29860, and the Haliburton collections, British Museum, Add MSS. 25613-25675.

FOUR

SINAI *and* JERUSALEM

Years in the Near East, under the benign action of the Mediterranean sun, had brought about an outward change in the appearance of Frederick Catherwood. He dressed as an Arab with robe and turban and, so says his friend Arundale, "he was well versed in Oriental manners." He could speak fluent Arabic, Italian, and Hebrew; he seems also to have lost something of the reticence that early characterized him. By 1833 he had accumulated a great mass of material and observations such as no architect-archaeologist had up until then — or perhaps since. He had traveled the classical lands, Italy, Greece, and Sicily, delineating all with considerable skill, and after his journeys on the Nile he had been employed for a while as an engineer by Mehemet Ali to repair the mosques at Cairo. This permitted him to make the first architectural analysis of Saracenic structures (although these drawings, unhappily, are lost). In favor with Mehemet Ali and carrying the Pasha's personal firman, he traveled through Libya into West Africa, and in 1832 he was at the Regency of Tunis at Dougga*, where he drew a twenty-foot plinth, a beau-

* Frederick Catherwood: Account of the Punico-Libyan Monument at Dougga and the Remains of an Ancient Structure at Bless near the site of Ancient Carthage. Trans. of the American Ethnological Society, New York, 1845 (vol. I).

The Giza pyramids as drawn by F. Catherwood (circa 1826). The pyramids belonged to Cheops, Chephren and Mycerinus, arranged in chronological order and descending order in size. The Great Sphinx lies below them. Br. Mus. Add. Ms. 29812. Contemporary photograph is by George Holton.

Dear Sir

I am sorry that I cannot leave the drawings of the Pyramids in a more perfect state. The only level I had unfortunately fell and broke before I had measured little more than half way up the Pyramid. As it could not be replaced at Cairo I was obliged to wait the arrival of Mr. Arundale to recommence operations and this joined to a violent attack of Ophthalmia will explain the reason of the fair drawings not being made. I however will finish them on my return to England fit for publication without further remuneration and I only regret that circumstances prevented my leaving them in a more perfect state. With kind words to Mrs. Hay believe me

dear Sir
yours very truly
J. Catherwood

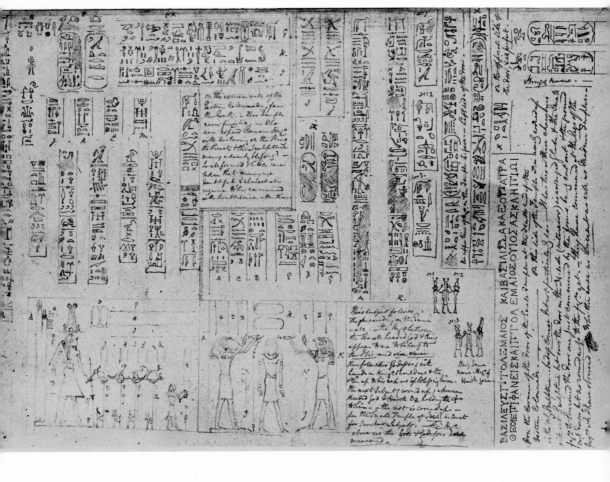

Valley of the Kings. Sketches and notes; "From the corner of the Door of the small
temple at the N/E end of Eastern Colonnade." Br. Mus. Add. Ms. 29847.

Letter from Catherwood (n.d.) to Robert Hay concerning his drawings of the Giza
pyramids. He mentions Arundale in the letter. Br. Mus. Add. Mss. 29859.

Three of Catherwood's *camera lucida* drawings of the Ramesseum II Court at Thebes, built by order of Rameses II (1301-1235 BC). Thebes was one of the greatest capital cities in antiquity — Homer's "Hundred-Gated-Thebes." These drawings were done with the aid of a *camera lucida*, a simple and effective device by which, using prism mirrors, the subject can rapidly be traced on paper. The light outline could later be shaded, a firmer line given to the rapid sketch or it could be made into a water color. The *camera lucida* explains the great mass of material that Catherwood could gather in a short time; it also explains his accuracy. Br. Mus. Add. Mss. 29816.

Thebes, the Ramesseum II Court; two *camera lucida* studies, slightly shaded. Opposite, and on the following spread Catherwood depicts the Temple of Isis and other related buildings on the island of Philae. These temples, now covered by the water of the artificial lake of the Aswan Dam will disappear completely when the new dam goes into operation. At the moment, for a few days in July the Temple of Isis appears from the depths of the water. The buildings were dedicated to Hathor, goddess of distant places, and the finest temple to Isis. Some of the last monuments are dated A D 473. Br. Mus. Add Mss. 29835.

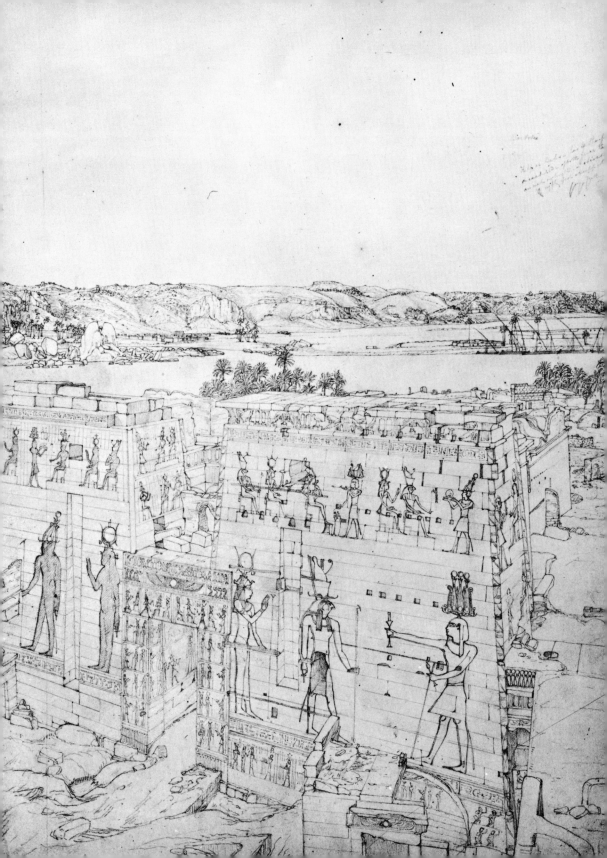

Edfu, Frederick Catherwood's *camera lucida* drawing of Edfu, an important city in
Upper Egypt. The Great Temple of Horus, begun by Ptolemy III in 237 B C and
finished 180 years later. Br. Mus. Add. Mss. 29832..

Detail of the Temple of Horus at Edfu, as photographed by George Holton. Contrast of *camera lucida* study and the photograph graphically exhibit the difficulties of the early archaeological explorers.

The Colossi of Memnon, a photograph by George Holton. The seventy-foot-high monuments were cut from reddish conglomerate rock quarried from the sand hills of Edfu and floated down the Nile in specially constructed barges. Even the architect-sculptor was awed by their size and grandeur. "They are wonderful," so he wrote in the glyphs, "for size and height and they will last as long as heaven."

The Colossi of Memnon; Catherwood's first *camera lucida* drawing of the two statues of Amen-hotep III, sketched in May, 1833. The two huge figures sit enthroned in solitude on the plains of Thebes, between Medinet Habu and the Ramesseum. Catherwood's greatest contribution to Egyptology was the excavation and minute study of the Colossi. Br. Mus. Robert Hay Add. Mss. 29829.

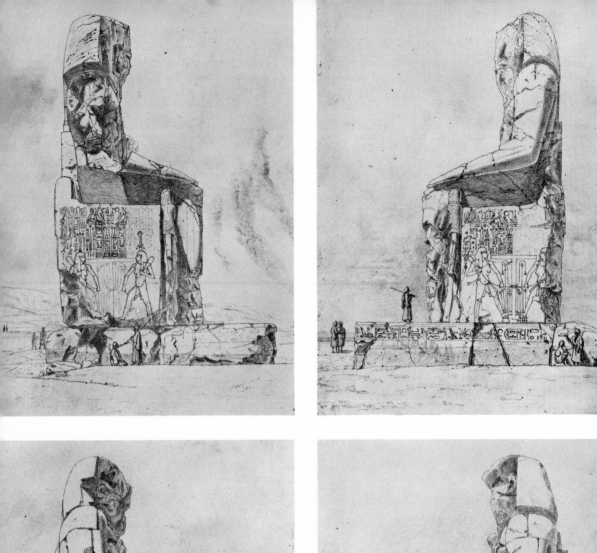

Catherwood's *camera lucida* drawing of the rear view of one of the Colossi. The hieroglyphs are so accurate that Egyptologists have no difficulty deciphering them. Left, side-view studies of the Colossi. At the foot of the page is the so-called "vocal" statue which was believed to emit a melodious tone at sunrise. Thus the image would offer sweet and plaintive greeting to his mother Eos as she made her appearance on earth at dawn. The goddess, hearing the sound, would shed her tears, (the morning dew) over her beloved son. Many travelers of old claimed to have heard the phenomenon. Others, among them the geographer Strabo, doubted its authenticity. The Emperor Hadrian (130 A D) together with a large retinue spent several days at the "singing" colossus. Br. Mus. Robert Hay Add. Mss. 29829.

Detail drawing of panel on the southwest side of the "not-vocal-statue," reproduced top left on preceding spread. Below is Catherwood's schematic drawing, restoration and excavation of the Colossi of Memnon. Catherwood made the first excavation of these monuments to discover that they rested on a sub-stratum of sand. Note his observations on the various silt deposits of the Nile in 1830, as he drew the monuments in 1833. Signed F. Catherwood. Br. Mus. Robert Hay Add. Mss. 29829.

tiful four-columned prostyle of the Corinthian order, built with an inscription on its facade to Ateban son of Lepmatath son of Palu, a numidian chieftain who died in the time of Massinissa in the last part of the 3rd century B.C. The ruins of Dougga left a profound impression on Catherwood.

In 1833 Catherwood, Arundale, and Bonomi, dressed as Turkish merchants, completed their preparations for an expedition into Sinai and Arabia Petra. They purchased, wrote Arundale, "necessaries from the bazaar at Cairo," and left for Mt. Sinai on August 29, 1833. With the published narrative of Arundale and the unpublished diary of Bonomi one can trace Catherwood's participation on this desert journey. They followed the camel-caravan route around the shore of the Red Sea. After leaving Suez, they passed hundreds of camels watering at Girgade, the nearest potable water to Suez. On the seventh day of travel they came to Wadi Mokateb — the Rock of Inscriptions. These inscriptions — in many languages, Greek, Arabic, and Latin — were "copied by Cath and Arundale."

The Sinai Peninsula is filled with ruins of ruins and in the Gebel el Igma, they came to the ruins of Sabit el Khadin — which they duly limned. Later, when the road reached 5,000 feet altitude, they came upon the ancient Ummlugma mines, where they found the furnaces which melted gold and copper for the predynastic Egyptian cultures. Many of the sites which lie midway between two cultures, Egyptian and Nabatean, were copied by Catherwood. On the 16th of September they arrived at the Convent of St. Catherine on Mt. Sinai. This Greek convent, famed for its hospitality for those who tested the aridities of Edom, was the guardian of Mt. Sinai, where Moses received the tablets from the hands of the Demiurge; Bonomi's dairy records: "Begun to ascend the mountain [we] made sketches of all the remarkable spots."

In a strange coincidence, which would have much to do with Catherwood's latter life and the discovery of the Maya civilization, John Lloyd Stephens followed the path of Catherwood to Mt. Sinai three years later. A New York lawyer, traveling for "reasons of health" throughout the world, Stephens had gone up the Nile in 1836 and later took the desert trail to the convent of St. Catherine. The lively description of his travels and his stay at the convent, which he wrote in *Incidents of Travel in Egypt and Arabia*

Petraea, was to cause Herman Melville to turn toward literature as a career and this concatenation of cause and effect was also to put Stephens in contact with Catherwood and — to continue this train of pre-established harmonies — to bring about the discovery of the Mayas.*

During the last days of September and into October 1833, Catherwood, Arundale, and Bonomi traveled through the classical desertic lands where, despite bouts of ague and illness ("Catherwood unwell so we tarried and Arundale had three attacks of his old complaint"), they continued to draw the remains of whatever came within sight. By the 6th of October they arrived in Jerusalem.

It was Jerusalem and its environs that inspired Catherwood to undertake the most important of his architectural-archaeological researches in the Middle East; he was to complete the entire plan and architectural details of El-'Aqsa — the Mosque of Omar, the Dome of the Rock.

Throughout October 1833 one can see, through the entries in the diary of Joseph Bonomi, the manner in which Frederick Catherwood was essaying the first approaches to the Jerusalem "problem"; "Catherwood and I walked all this afternoon round the walls and returning by the pilgrims' gate. . . Monday 14th. . . put into effect two views of the house of Lazarus and the via Dolorosa. . . Monday 21st. . . sketching the Dome [of the Rock] and an outline of those strangely twisted columns. . ."

Within days they were being troubled by Arabs who told them that they were not allowed "to draw within the sacred enclosure. Cath went yesterday and the Governor saw him. . ." Later "Cath was within the wall. . . he is now so bold that I think I must make my escape. . ."

By the 24th of October Catherwood had set his materials and "apparati" on the roof of the House of Pontius Pilate and Bonomi noted:

* *Maya Explorer: Life of John Lloyd Stephens,* by Victor W. von Hagen. University of Oklahoma Press, 1947.
Incidents of Travel in Yucatan, by John L Stephens. Edited with introduction and notes by Victor W. von Hagen, 2 vols. University of Oklahoma Press, 1963.
Incidents of Travel in Egypt and Arabia Petraea, by John L. Stephens (originally published in 1837). Edited with life, introduction, and notes by Victor W. von Hagen, 2 vols. University of Oklahoma Press, 1968.

"Cath is making his Panorama of Jerusalem." Working with his camera lucida* Catherwood was able, by this simple yet effective instrument, to put down relatively quickly the entire outline of Jerusalem, as if he was using a fish-eye lense in a modern camera. He then set about to make a portfolio of drawings of each important building. From these, in 1835, Robert Burford was able, with Catherwood's aid, to make a huge circular mural of Jerusalem. It was first exhibited in Leicester Square, London, in 1835. The mural itself, as it was illuminated by gaslight, was destroyed by fire; all that is left of it, to gain some idea of what it was, is the pamphlet *Description of a View of the City of Jerusalem Painted from Drawings. . . by Frederick Catherwood* (London 1835) with a woodcut of the mural itself and with identifications of figures and buildings portrayed in the mural. It was fully detailed, from a prospect of the Dead Sea to the historical places within the walled city. In a rare autobiographical gesture under No. 45 of the key to the mural there was: "Messrs. Catherwood and Bonomi", pictured sitting under a large umbrella — indistinct in the wood-cut — apparently under the Arch of Ecce Homo in the Via Dolorosa.

Later Catherwood brought this Panorama to New York and opened his own rotunda; advertisements in the New York papers announced:

> "A Painting of the largest class, 10,000 square feet from drawings by Mr. Catherwood brilliantly illuminated every evening by up-wards of 200 gas-lights, admission 25 cents."

The New York *Mirror*'s critic was ecstatic. "Nothing can surpass the style in which Jerusalem is before us. . ." Nor was the revenue of the Panorama lessened by the praise that Stephens gave it in the 10th edition of his *Incidents;* ". . . the author would endeavor to direct the attention of the public to Mr. Catherwood's panorama of Jerusalem. . . exhibited in an area of nearly ten thousand feet erected for its exhibition. . ." The Panorama continued successfully in New York for six years when misfortune, which

---

* The camera lucida was an instrument, much used in the ninetenth century, for copying the outlines of buildings. By means of a series of prisms, formed by a certain arrangement of lenses, it causes an external image to be projected on a sheet of paper; outlines can be faithfully traced.

always seemed to be in attendance upon Frederick Catherwood, moved again: Jerusalem was utterly destroyed.*

As a corollary to his work on the Panorama, Catherwood drew, as he was also a surveyor, a map of Jerusalem which he thought sufficiently important to have lithographed and published.** It became another link that brought Stephens and Catherwood together.

After the Panorama, Frederick Catherwood concentrated on making a detailed study of the Dome of the Rock. When the Arabs swept into the Jordan Valley, overwhelming the armies of Heraclitus, all Palestine fell. The Arabs entered Jerusalem A.D. 640. Behind the ancient city wall — the lower courses of which belonged to the period of Herod the Great — the Arabs, with the aid of Greek Christian architects and workmen, erected the magnificent Dome of the Rock. It and the adjoining Mosque of El-'Aqsa were built in A. D. 691 by the Umayyad Caliph Al Malik.

The Dome of the Rock had long been a subject of heated dispute between contending antiquarians, architects, and religious historians. A mosaic-walled mosque in a corner of ancient Jerusalem, it has long held a place in the Islamic diadem, for here Mohammed ascended on his eagle-winged horse to visit the seven heavens of Islam. Mohammed's footprint is supposed to be impressed in that sacred black rock, a fact on which Mark Twain cast much impish doubt when he measured it and judged that

* 31 July, 1842, Philip Hone's dairy: "Catherwood's Panorama of Jerusalem [was] burnt last evening... This will be a severe loss... to science and the arts in general. The edifice being perfectly circular without windows... the contents of a peculiarly in-flammable nature... the conflagration was like a huge cauldron." The New York *Herald*: "The Fire at Catherwood's.. is likely to prove more disastrous than we at first anticipated.. He was insured for only $3,000; his private loss will be at least $20,000 more."

** F Catherwood: Plan of Jerusalem, published August 1, 1835; F. Catherwood, 21 Charles Sq., Hoxton, London. Of this Stephens wrote in his *Incidents*, "I was fortunate to find [in 1836] a lithographic map made by Mr. Catherwood... and which I found a better guide to all the interesting localities than any other I could procure in Jerusalem."

36

Mohammed would have taken a size 18 shoe. In Catherwood's time, unbelievers took their lives in their hands when they entered. No architect up to that time had ever limned it nor its interior design.

This smoldering Arab resentment against them seemed to have been transferred to their own lives; Joseph Bonomi complains in his diary: "This evening poor Arundale fell down [epilepsy] we. . . applied our usual remedy, cold water thrown from a height on his head. . . at 12 o'clock another attack." Next day, Arundale being now well, they both went out together to measure and draw Absalom's tomb. On the 13th of October it was Catherwood; "I had a row with Cath. . . his conduct always appeared ungenerous and in some cases unjust. . . I have as he says formed so bad an opinion of him that we propose to separate at Beirut." The quarrel was still going on two days later; "I have never had for these eight years [on the Nile, in Egypt, and in the desert] so disagreeable a day as this, perhaps my own doing having told Cath my clear opinion of him. . ."

The reasons for this quarrel are not given, but there is evidence of this recurrent spleen elsewhere. Later in Yucatán, even in the easy and informal style of Stephens, there appear veiled hints of some fundamental disequilibrium in Catherwood's character. There must be some reasons why he was never portrayed by his contemporaries; he is always Mr. Catherwood, sometimes "F.C." and rarely "Cath". Of autobiography there is little; he refers to himself in latter life as "a sober, plodding old fellow. . ." He made, as told, a self-portrait of himself in the Panorama of Jerusalem which is destroyed, and certainly drew his own likeness in 1842 in a blurred self-portrait measuring the Maya ruins at Tulum in Yucatán. Catherwood only appears as a shadowy and indistinct figure moving against a sharply detailed background of persons and places; as a person he seems to have as much substance as Banquo's ghost although he was the model of Walter Hartwright, of Wilkie Collins's *The Woman in White,* who goes off to Central America in the 1850's to make architectural illustrations for an archaeological expedition.

What was the demon that drove Catherwood? Whatever there *was* about him or was not, he had, in all his adversity, a single-minded drive to complete his archaeological studies. By November 7th he is again at the

Dome of the Rock despite the threat if he continued his drawing. "Cath said he would go in even if it were necessary to say he was a Mussulman." Then, on November 13th, 1833, Catherwood dressed as an Egyptian officer and carrying, as he wrote, "a strong firman expressly naming me as an engineer in the service of Mehemet Ali," he again entered the mosque. In this instance Catherwood left a personal account. After making a survey of Jerusalem and a general plan of Harm es Shereef, and drawings of the exteriors of El-'Aqsa and the Dome of the Rock, he entered the interior of the mosque "feeling irresistibly urged to make an attempt."

"... It was a proceeding certain to attract attention and expose me to dangerous consequences. The cool assurance of my servant, at once befriended and led me on. We entered, and arranging the camera [lucida] I quickly sat down to my work, not without some nervousness... However, most of them passed on, deceived by my dress and the quiet indifference with which I regarded them. At length some, more fanatic than the rest, began to think all could not be right; they gathered at a distance in groups, suspiciously eyeing me, and comparing notes with one another; a storm was evidently gathering. They approached, broke into sudden clamour and surrounding me, uttered loud curses; their number increased most alarmingly, and with their numbers their menacing language and gestures. Escape was hopeless; I was completely surrounded by a mob of two hundred people who seemed screwing up their courage for a sudden rush upon me. Nothing could be better than the conduct of Suleyman, my servant, at this crisis; affecting vast indignation at the interruption, he threatened to inform the Governor, out-hectored the most clamorous, and raising his whip, actually commenced a summary attack upon them, and knocked off the cap of one of the holy dervishes. This brought matters to a crisis; and, I believe, few moments would have passed ere we had been torn to pieces, when an incident occurred that converted our danger and discomfiture into positive triumph. This was the sudden appearance of the Governor on the steps of the platform, accompanied by his usual train. Catching sight of him, the foremost — those I mean who had been disgraced by the blows of Suleyman — rushed tumultuously up to him, demanding the punishment of the infidel, who was profaning the holy precincts, and horse-whipping the true believers. At this the Governor drew near, and as we had often smoked together, and were well acquainted, he saluted me politely, and supposing it to be beyond the reach of possibility that I could venture to do what I was about without a warrant from the pasha, he at once applied himself to cool the rage of the mob. 'You see, my friends,' he said, 'that our holy mosque is in a dilapidated state, and no doubt our lord and master Mehemet Ali has sent this Effendi to survey it, in order to complete its repair. If we are unable to do these things for ourselves, it is right to employ those who can; and such being the will of our lord, the pasha, I require you to disperse and not incur my displeasure by any further interruption.' And turning to me, he said, in hearing of them all, that if anyone had the hardihood to disturb me in the future, he would deal in a summary way with him. I did not, of course, think it necessary to undeceive the worthy Governor; and gravely thanking him, proceeded with my drawing. All went on quietly after this.

"During six weeks, I continued to investigate every part of the mosque and its precincts, introducing my astonished companions as necessary assistants in the work of the survey. But when I heard of the near approach of *Ibrahim Pasha,* I thought it was time to take leave of Jerusalem. . ."

Thus Catherwood, with the assistance of Arundale and Bonomi, finished the drawings of the mosque. They made sections of the Dome measuring the exterior wall, and within six weeks Catherwood had enough details of the most famous mosque in the whole Mohammedan world to erect another like it. It was, until that time, Catherwood's greatest single effort. He had intended on his return to London to publish his work in book form, utilizing all the superb drawings that he had made. He found the London publishers indifferent; in disgust Catherwood put his drawings away. Not many years after Catherwood had worked there, a violent controversy developed between various schools of architecture over the origin of the Dome of the Rock. Mr. James Fergusson, the eminent historian of architecture, conjectured that this mosque had been built by Constantine, over the tomb of Christ. Challenged by antiquarians, he sought out Catherwood, to see the drawings and prove his archaeological theory. In 1846 he made contact with him: "The only means," Fergusson wrote, "that occurred to me of getting out of this dilemma was trying if possible to gain access to Mr. Catherwood's drawings which I knew from the works of Dr. Robinson and Mr. [W.H.] Bartlett did exist somewhere. Mr. Catherwood was then in Demerara [British Guiana] and in answer to a letter I wrote him he gave me hope he would accede to my wishes when he returned to his country which he did last autumn [1846] . . ." In January 1847 Catherwood turned over his collection of drawings to Fergusson and persuaded Francis Arundale, who was on the point of death, to do likewise; "They agreed," acknowledged James Fergusson, "to turn over the material in a handsome manner." Thus disappeared one other phase of Catherwood's own archaeological monument; he lost his identity. Now all his drawings of the Mosque of Omar have disappeared.

JARASH, BAALBEK, *and* PALMYRA

CATHERWOOD, after his harrowing weeks in the interior of the Mosque of Omar, was anxious to see those ruins — not less than fifty miles from Jerusalem — that had been discovered by the German traveler Ulrich Seetzen in 1806. The usual group, Catherwood, Arundale, and Bonomi, set off for Jarash, located in the present day Kingdom of Jordan.

At the end of a "beautiful day," as Bonomi's diary expresses itself, on the way to Jarash, they stayed in a mosque. "Found there a Turkish soldier whom we invited to supper with us. Arundale fell ill, two fits before morning, what with that and the fleas and the smoke got no sleep at all. . ."

The diary marked the next one "another fine day." The three began bargaining over transportation — an eternal problem — to go to the Roman ruins. "This morning [Sunday 8th of November] made a bargain for four mules to take us to Jarash. . . Cath bought a nice little horse. . . for 300 piasters." And mounted on that "little horse" Catherwood rode into Jarash.

Under its Roman name, Gerasa, it was one of the members of the Greek commercial league known as the Decapolis. The Romans, when they rebuilt the city and incorporated it into Provincia Arabia, wisely allowed the Greek culture and language to remain. The Emperor Vespasian had erected a wall around it in 75 A.D., and through it flowed a perennial stream, making the land about it vividly green. It gave it an arcadian setting. Jarash is the finest and best preserved Roman provincial city in the middle east, the Roman road passes through a triumphal arch, runs aside the ruins of a hippodrome and then leads into an immense irregularly elliptical Forum; it is fully unique. The road, which becomes the principal street of Jarash was colonnaded from one end to the other. The original pavingstones — the polished white limestone slabs — still lie in their original form wonderfully engineered with a drainage system underneath. Shops once lined the streets; a nymphaeum, lovingly created to receive and then dispense the water of a brook which flowed into it, still stands mid-distance in the street. There are two theaters with Greek inscriptions, one at each end of the city; temples, baths, and a scattering of house sites. It seems incredible that this city should have slipped from memory until the German traveler Seetzen came across it in 1806.

Catherwood tried to work rapidly within the time at their disposal, but there were problems. Bonomi: "I made a sketch or two, found the people [of Jarash] extremely troublesome so I returned. . ." Catherwood, in order to dominate the situation, showed his famous gun [the one with the seven barrels]. The Arabs, wanting to know how it could be fired without a flint, fell down prostrate when it went off. Bonomi's mule bolted "so that I was obliged to offer ten piasters to some Arabs to catch him." Then there was Arundale; epileptic fits came on now with greater frequency and most of Catherwood's time was spent attending him. Arundale showed "symptoms of mental derangement. . . every person we met he said were banditti, wanted Cath to shoot them. . ." Under these circumstances there was not too much archaeological rendering.

And yet Catherwood made the first ground plan. As all else it was never published but lay entombed in the Robert Hay collections. He also made a drawing of the Temple of Artemis — perhaps the first ever made by a capable artist. This had reasonable recognition; it was engraved by Finden for his *Landscape Illustrations of the Bible* (London 1836).

It was inevitable that Catherwood would be drawn to the ruins of Baalbek. A pass through the mountains inland from Beirut led to the verdant valley that lay between Lebanon and Anti-Lebanon, fertile and well watered from snow-covered peaks that surrounded it. The Orontes River had its origin place there and it was famed for its cult of the god Baal. It had been Phoenician, then Greek, and finally Roman, but retained its Greek name, Heliopolis, the Sun City. Under the Antonines the Romans lavished much attention upon it; the huge complex of the temples of Baalbek rose from the ruins of early Phoenician structures. The Temple of Bacchus rested upon monolithic cut limestone; the largest single piece of stone ever cut, transported and fitted into place, was sixty feet long, seventeen feet across, the weight of each stone was 1,500 tons. On this base the Temple of Bacchus rose.

Pitching his tent among the fallen columns, Catherwood, with Arundale in attendance, began the survey of the Temple of Jupiter. Giving careful attention to detail Catherwood drew the architectural lyrics of Baalbek, the Propylaea, the forecourt, the Great Forecourt with its altar pristinely classical, the Temple of Jupiter-Baal, and sections of the Temple of Bacchus with its exquisite stone doorway and motif of fig leaves that time and man had spared. It had been erected in the era of Antoninus Pius (86-161), pillaged in 748 by the Seljuks, fell in 1134 into the bloodstained hands of Genghis Khan, and was taken by the Turks in 1517, in whose territory it remained until 1918.

The six remaining columns of the Temple of Jupiter, 62 feet in height, commanded a panorama of the watered greensward. The beautiful Roman temple, which had been turned into a basilica by the Byzantines, transformed by the Moslems into a mosque, and destroyed by the Mongols, was now only winter stalls for nomadic shepherds. There remained only six pillars, still retaining architrave, frieze, and cornice. Composed of three immense marble drums, the columns had been cemented by molten lead. This led to their destruction, for Arabs tumbled the columns to obtain the lead. The stupendous ruins have been figured and described over and over again. The author of *South Wind*, the late Norman Douglas, even used it as a setting for an unfinished novel, *Love Among the Ruins*. It had been known to the British ever since Robert Wood published, in 1753, *The Ruins of Baalbek*.

There is no other reference to Frederick Catherwood's visit to

Baalbek than passing reference by Arundale who accompanied him. All else we know about Catherwood's work in Baalbek is bibliographical.*

On the 16th of March, 1834, as we know from a letter dated from Damascus, Frederick Catherwood was preparing to go to Palmyra. This fabled desert city, first seen by Englishmen in the 17th century, lay 125 miles southeast from Damascus directly in the desert. Since Palmyra was an oasis and offered a perennial water supply it was an important station on the caravan traffic route. The Roman road enters Palmyra through the gateway of the great wall of Justinian, built in the 6th century A.D. At once one enters the long colonnaded street of which 150 columns remain standing. As at Jarash, the street of white limestone proceeds between the columns. A water conduit ran beside the road and it still can be seen ramifying into buildings which were the residential center. A well-preserved theater, only the seats being weathered by wind and sun, is directly beside the road, and around it a whole city of shops, residences, fountains, temples and caravanserais. These give an impression of the wealth of the city that governed the vast caravan trade with the East.

Palmrya acquired its pre-eminence in trade and power in Trajan's time. It became a desert emporium. Cotton was brought into it by bales, golden trinkets from Parthia, jewels from Babylon, and silk dyed with Tyrian purple; there were myrrh from Ethiopia, rare woods and spices from Persa, richly woven textiles, and birds.

In a lively letter to Joseph Bonomi, dated 16th March, 1834, Catherwood asks him "to join us in an excursion to Palmyra. We hear from Sheriff Bay that the road is safe and intend to leave as soon as possible after the return of the messenger. . ." Catherwood's drawings of Palmyra have disappeared, as have the drawings and the Panorama of Damascus.

The Panorama of Damascus he must have done within the same period because he writes: "At present [the month of March] the trees are not out and consequently I cannot begin my Panorama." That it was completed we know from the puff that John L. Stephens gave his Rotunda in

* Robert Burford: Description of a View of the Ruins of The Temple at Baalbek... Painted from drawings by F. Catherwood. London 1844.

44

his book. "Catherwood... has under his control large panoramas [in New York] of Jerusalem, Thebes, Damascus, Baalbek, Algiers, Carthage, and Athens." Since Catherwood lived in all these cities it is apparent that he did make panoramas of them all. And all are lost.

Suddenly a Mrs. Catherwood emerges. The "we" in his Damascus letter is Mrs. Catherwood. Presumably they were married early in 1834, for he wrote, "I have much more attention paid to me now when I am married." His wife lived with him in New York (466 Houston Street), for Catherwood's Day Book for his Rotunda, now in the collections of the New York Historical Society, shows that his partner, while he was in London, "paid Mrs. Catherwood twenty dollars a week." And when Catherwood was exploring in Yucatán it was agreed between Stephens and himself that "a payment of twenty-five dollars per week should be made to Mrs. Catherwood and family [two sons]." In 1849 still looking for the financial security that eluded him, Catherwood wrote to Stephens: "... it is absolutely necessary that I should be doing something for my children are growing up around me. . ." And yet there are no names mentioned and there is no record of his family. On Catherwood's death one of his family put his library, his various instruments, including the far-famed *camera lucida* and other memorabilia — up for auction. On December 1, 1856, one year after he had disappeared in the icy grey waters of the Atlantic, Puttick and Simpson, autioneers, put all up for sale. Dispersed, burnt and lost — it is as if some spiteful poltergeist had followed in Catherwood's wake destroying every page of his life's testimony and leaving the greatest of the pioneer architect-archaeologists sunk in the stream of time.

SIX

The MAYAS *and*
The VIEWS *of* ANCIENT MONUMENTS

FREDERICK CATHERWOOD arrived in New York in 1836, at the urging of John L. Stephens, and immediately set about as an architect, a panoramist, and a lecturer. While these varied professions were being carried out Catherwood carried on fevered conversations with Stephens about archaeology.

John Lloyd Stephens referred to himself as a New Yorker, yet in fact he had been born in 1805 in Shrewsbury, New Jersey. He had attended Columbia College and set off to read law for a year at Tapping Reeve's Law School in Connecticut. Then, before he hung out his law-shingle, he made an adventurous tour of the western prairies in 1824, going down the entire length of the Mississippi. In 1835, being unable to practice law because of a persistent streptococcal throat infection, he left for Europe "for reasons of health." Stephens made the Grand Tour — Paris, Rome, Salerno, Greece, then to Smyrna in Turkey. Then, no longer for "reasons of health," he traveled from Odessa to Moscow and by a *kibitka* conveyance to Poland.

In 1835 while in Paris and waiting to find a passage home, he happened to look through — and buy — a copy of Léon de Laborde's *Voyage de l'Arabie Petrée,* illustrated with fascinating lithographs of the ancient city called Petra.

On January 1, 1836, "with a fair wind and the Star-spangled Banner (made by an Arab tailor) flapping in the wind," Stephens was wafted up the Nile. Three months later he was following Catherwood's trail to Sinai, Jordan, and then to Jerusalem. Catherwood's map guided him while he was there and when he was in London he visited the Panoramas — thus Stephens and Catherwood met.

On his return to New York in 1836, Stephens had written two books,* both successful. The one on his travels in Arabia Petraea was reviewed by Edgar Allan Poe who wrote that it was "the most interesting book on travel ever published in the English language." It passed through ten editions in four years. Having made $25,000 from his book within two years, Stephens — the law now forgotten — was in a financial position to make a proposal to Frederick Catherwood for an exploration of the vague and dimly heard ancient cities in Central America.

It is an historical fact that in 1838 only three archaeological sites were known in the Maya area: Copán in Honduras, Palenque, three hundred miles to the northeast in Chiapas, Mexico, and Uxmal, of equal distance north from the ruin in Yucatán. No one ascribed these widely scattered cities to one culture; the word "Maya" in connection with them was unknown.

Stephens made his decision, as he no longer had to depend on financial assistance from his father, for his two books, continuing from edition to edition, were earning magnificent royalties. He was now ready to put into operation the plans that he and Catherwood had long ago formulated. "Fortunately [for Stephens]," writes John R. Bartlett in his journal,

"Mr. Catherwood. . . with whom he was on intimate terms, was then in New York. Mr. Catherwood had great enthusiasm

*Incidents of Travel in Egypt, Arabia Petraea and the Holy Land, 2 vols. Harper & Bros., New York, 1837.
Incidents of Travel in Greece, Turkey, Russia and Poland, 2 vols. Harper & Bros., New York, 1838.

47

in anything pertaining to architecture, and was an ardent lover of the picturesque and of archaeological researches. Mr. Stephens made him a favorable offer to accompany him to Central America, which offer he at once accepted."

As this historic contract between Stephens and Catherwood has recently come to light, it is enlightening to read the whole of it:

"Memorandum of an agreement made this day [September 9, 1839] between John L. Stephens and Frederick Catherwood. Frederick Catherwood agrees to accompany the said Stephens on his journey to Central America, and to continue and remain with the said Stephens until the said Stephens shall finish his official duties with the government of Central America, and then to accompany the said Stephens on a tour through the provinces of Chiapas and Yucatán, and that he, the said Catherwood, will throughout the said tour exercise his skill as an artist and make drawings of the ruins of Palenque, Uxmal, Copán and such other ruined cities, places, scenes and monuments as may be considered desirable by the said Stephens, and that he will keep and preserve the said drawings to be engraved or otherwise made use of by the said Stephens for the sole use and benefit of the said Stephens, until released from his obligation by the said Stephens; and that he will not publish directly or indirectly the said drawings, nor any narration of the incidents of his journey, nor any description of places or persons, and that he will not in any way interfere with the right of the said Stephens to the absolute and exclusive use of all the information, drawings and material collected on the said journey. And in consideration of the above, the said Stephens agrees to pay the traveling expenses of the said Catherwood from the time of his departure from New York until his return thereto and the said Stephens stipulates that the said Catherwood shall make and realize out of the materials collected on the said journey and at the disposal of the said Stephens the sum of one thousand and five hundred dollars within one year after the return of the

Karnak, F. Catherwood's rapidly executed sketch made by using a *camera lucida*.
Site unidentified, probably one of the Halls of Amun. Karnak lay on the right side
of the Nile across from Thebes. Br. Mus., Robert Hay Add. Mss. 29826.

Karnak is famous for its superfluity of obelisks. They date back to predynastic times
when the upright stone had the first light of the rising sun. Br. Mus., Robert Hay
Add. Mss. 29826. Opposite page: The great obelisk at Karnak at the Pillar of
Tuthmosis III. The rude stone, quarried from red granite at Aswan, weighed hundreds of tons, was floated down the river, carved, and erected. Br. Mus., Robert
Hay Add. Mss. 29814. In the comparison photograph, by George Holton, the visible
obelisk face corresponds to the left face in Catherwood's drawing.

Catherwood's *camera lucida* sketch of the Gateway of Evergestes I, Karnak. The hyptostyle-hall of Rameses temple of Amun. Karnak had the largest assembly of temples in Egypt. Enlarged through generations of pharaohs from the Middle Kingdom to the time of the Romans. Br. Mus., Robert Hay Add. Mss. 29826.

Catherwood's unsigned watercolor of a scene at Karnak. Br. Mus. Robert Hay Add. Mss., 29839. It is interesting to contrast this free-hand sketch with the drawing on the opposite page, made by first shading, then coloring, a *camera lucida* drawing.

Watercolor drawing of the Temple of Hathor, at Dendera, built in the first century B C. Dendera, opposite Coptos on the Nile, was the capital of the 6th nome, or province, of the Kingdom of Upper Egypt. Br. Mus. Robert Hay Add. Mss., 29814.

Frederick Catherwood (self-portrait) measuring the Maya ruins of Tulum, Quintana Roo, Mexico. That this is Catherwood is deduced from the fact that there were only three white men on the expedition. In the larger print Dr. Cabot can be seen going off to hunt bird specimens, left of the ruins. Stephens in a short blue jacket and Panama hat pulls one end of a measuring tape. The third and final figure is that of Frederick Catherwood. Although indistinct, it is the only known portrait of Catherwood. From Plate XXIV, *Views of Ancient Monuments*, London, 1844.

Broken Idol at Copán. Stele C. at the Maya ruins of Copán, Honduras. Erected 652 A D (12 Ahau 13 Kayab). Of it Catherwood wrote: "It is equal to the best remains of Egyptian art." The original sketch made at Copán in 1839. Sepia. Courtesy Henry Schnackenberg, Newtown, Conn.

The Well of Bolonchén, Yucatán. All rivers in Yucatán flowed underground and water had to be obtained from deep wells or cenotes. Bolonchén, the "village of the nine wells". The ladder illustrated by Catherwood was eighty feet long. The original sepia watercolor, owned by Henry Schnackenberg, Newtown, Conn.

The "Nunnery" at Uxmal, Yucatán. Catherwood's original drawing of the entire south facade of the quadrangle at Uxmal. This is low-built and heavily decorated with the motif of Itzamma, the long-nosed god. The original, of which only eight survive of the hundreds that were once in Catherwood's portfolio, is in the Museum of the American Indian, New York. Courtesy: Heye Foundation, Museum of the American Indian.

The "Nunnery," Uxmal. Catherwood's original sepia drawing of the entire south ☞ facade of the quadrangle at Uxmal. This is low-built and heavily decorated with the motif of Itzamma, the long-nosed god. The original, of which only eight survive of the hundreds that were once in Catherwood's portfolio, is a detail of a lithograph in *Views of Ancient Monuments*.

The House of the Magician, Uxmal, Yucatán. Original sepia drawing. This is a truncated Maya pyramid 80 feet high that shadows the Nunnery quadrangle at Uxmal. The doorway is actually a gigantic stone-laid mask, 12 feet square. Its open mouth is the doorway. The temple is reached by climbing 240 stone steps. There is a stairway on both sides of the temple. A detail of the doorway as used for a lithograph in Catherwood's *Views of Ancient Monuments*.

Yum Kax, Lord of Harvest, Maya ruins of Copán. Original sepia drawing. Owned ☞ by Mr. Henry Schnackenberg, Newtown, Conn.

The well and temple at Zabaché, Yucatán. Late Maya, League of Mayapán. The structure is 20 feet long and 10 feet high, built with roof-comb characteristic of late Maya architecture. Compare the original engraving with the lithograph from *Views of Ancient Monuments,* improved upon by placing the cenote in front of the temple rather than behind it for "artistic effect."

said Stephens and Catherwood to the said city — and in case said sum shall not be so realized the said Stephens agrees to pay the same in cash — or else in lieu of the said sum of $1500 the said Stephens will deliver for Mr. Catherwood's benefit an introductive lecture or two lectures in one, two or three courses of lectures on the antiquities of Central America, and whether the said Stephens shall deliver the said lecture or lectures or not shall be agreed upon and determined by and between the said Stephens and Catherwood after their return to this city.

"And the said Stephens further agrees that he will make provision for the payment of twenty-five dollars per week to Mrs. Catherwood and family during the absence of said Catherwood; it being understood that all the money which shall so be paid to Mrs. Catherwood and family shall be deducted from the abovesaid sum of $1500 or otherwise taken into the amount of a final settlement as so much money paid to the said Catherwood.

"New York — September 1839

"Received two hundred dollars on account of the above sum of fifteen hundred. F.C."

The next recorded date is November 17, 1839, and it is a memorable one in America archaeological history, for it was on that day that Catherwood and Stephens stood before the jungle-covered remains of Copán. "I am entering," Stephens recalled later, "abruptly upon new ground." And so they were. While Stephens directed the clearing of the forest, Catherwood put up his easel and came to grips for the first time with Maya art. "As we feared," wrote Stephens of his companion's efforts, "the designs were so intricate and complicated, the subjects so entirely new and unintelligible, that he had great difficulty in drawing."

In the end Catherwood succeeded, and so well that a century later an American archaeologist looking at these pictures made at Copán in 1839 wrote that "his drawing. . . is so accurate that it is possible to decipher the date inscribed on it." After finding more thitherto unknown ruins in Guatemala, they went on to Palenque, in the jungles of Chiapas, Mexico. The two explorers would have gone on to find more cities in Yucatán if malaria had not laid Catherwood low; as it was, their first look at Maya civilization had been decisive.

Within less than a year of their return to New York, Stephens's first book, *Incidents of Travel in Central America, Chiapas, and Yucatán*, with its wonderful Catherwood engravings, was ready for the press. Edgar Allan Poe, reviewing it for *Graham's Magazine* (and he was the only critic who really had anything significant to say about it as a book), wrote that it was a "magnificent one." In the autumn of 1841, hardly giving themselves time to savor their success (the book went through eight editions in three years), Stephens and Catherwood were again in Yucatán. Now there were three, for Dr. Samuel Cabot of Boston, physician and ornithologist, had joined them. This time their archaeological researches were confined to the Yucatán peninsula, and it was quite enough. Within less than a year they found forty-four Maya sites and laid the base, for all time, of the history of Maya culture.

Among the greatest of the cities that Stephens and Catherwood discovered and recorded, in the dry-jungle interior and along the wind-swept north coast, was Uxmal, without doubt one of the most architecturally uniform and consistently beautiful cities in the entire Maya realm. Catherwood made many detailed drawings of it; one of them, over eight feet in length, showing the intricate facade of the Nunnery Quadrangle, is to be seen in the Museum of the American Indian, New York. Numerous other originals attest to Catherwood's skill as an architectural draftsman.

On June 17, 1842, the expedition ended. The three men set sail for New York loaded down with Catherwood's drawings, Stephens's notes, and Cabot's stuffed birds and with numerous objects taken from the ruins as well. The owners — there was then no official protection of the ruins — gladly allowed this. These sculptures were the first to be seen outside of their place of origin, and it was Stephens's plan to see them made the basis of a museum for American antiquities.

In July of the same year these pieces of Maya pottery and carved, dated wooden lintels, from the ruins of Kabah and Uxmal were put on exhibit at Catherwood's Rotunda, along with hundreds of his large sepia drawings. The public scarcely had time to see them, however, for on the night of July 31, 1842, the Rotunda caught fire. Philip Hone, the New York merchant whose Pepysian diary is a shrewd, opinionated record of all that took place in those times, was himself a witness:

"Catherwood's Panorama of Thebes and Jerusalem burnt last evening about ten o'clock and those two valuable paintings were destroyed together with the other contents of the building, among which were a large collection of curiosities and relics. . . collected by Messrs. Stephens and Catherwood in their recent travels. . . This will be a severe loss. . . to science and the arts in general."

The New York *Herald* on the following day recorded that the building and its contents were totally destroyed and estimated their value at $23,000. Catherwood and his partner Jackson were not the sole sufferers. There was also Stephens who had brought back the Maya remains at so great a personal sacrifice; he especially grieved for the great carved wood lintel, decorated with the glyphs that would have told the date of the Kabah structure. "I had," he said, poking among the ruins the morning after, "the melancholy satisfaction of seeing their ashes exactly as the fire had left them."

Nonetheless, the financial disaster did not prevent Catherwood from going to work at once on the illustrations for their second book on the Mayas. Stephens had written it at great speed, despite the fact that it was more demanding than the book which had preceded it. While he gave his readers a full share of the "incidents," he now had to enter the unknown and uncertain ground of Maya history. It is amazing how capably Stephens handled all its contradictions, and this in the face of the numerous antiquarians who insisted these were not American Indian remains at all, but the work of various old world cultures.

In March of 1843, Harper & Brothers published the two-volume *Incidents of Travel in Yucatán,* containing 800 pages with 124 engravings from the drawings of Frederick Catherwood. Its success was immediate and in great measure paved the way for Prescott's *Conquest of Mexico,* which was soon to follow. Inevitably it led Stephens and Catherwood to think of publishing still another book, planned on so monumental a scale that only Audubon's vast folio *Birds of America* would have surpassed it. They planned to issue by subscription "a great work on American antiquities to contain 100 or 120 engravings folio — to be issued in four numbers quarterly, Price: $100!" This Stephens confided to William Prescott in a letter in March, 1843, asking Prescott to give them a text. The latter replied by return mail: "The *American Antiquities.* . . is a noble enterprise, and I hope it may find patronage. . . I will supply an article of the length you propose." Similar acceptances came from Humboldt and Albert Gallatin [on American Indian languages], and Catherwood even applied to his old friend from their Egyptian days, Sir John Wilkinson, to do a piece on the resemblance or dissimilarity of "American signs and symbols and those of Egypt."

But they were not to have an easy time of it. New York was in a period of political and economic uncertainty. Harper & Brothers, who had mined such gold from Stephens's publications, stalled for a while and then stated to the press that they were "not willing to undertake so great a work without some prospect of remuneration." Bartlett & Welford, the well-known booksellers, then took up the idea and displayed Catherwood's Maya drawings at their store in the Astor House on Broadway. But nothing came of it, and so Catherwood decided to try his luck in England.

Again he went from publisher to publisher, without success. "The booksellers say that trade is bad, etc., the old story and I fear a very true one. . . I have not yet attained my object, an audience of the Queen and Prince Albert. . . [but even this] ill accords with my *loco foco notions.* . ." At last Catherwood lost his illusions, and Stephens, for reasons unknown, withdrew. But it would not have been like Catherwood to let the "great project" die. He lowered his sights, reduced the plan to one within his own modest range. "I shall be my own Publisher."

He chose twenty-five drawings out of the 120, gave these to six of England's best lithographers, and prepared the text himself. On April 25, 1844, he published his one book:*Views of Ancient Monuments in Central America, Chiapas and Yucatán*, a series of twenty-five folio, hand-colored lithographs, limited to three hundred sets and dedicated to John L. Stephens. It was in its way a success, not as much of a one as Catherwood had originally wanted, yet sets were purchased and praised, and their influence was enormous.

The surprise — or it should have been — was the text. Catherwood was not a writer, even though he had done an occasional article on Mediterranean archaeology. Yet the calm, judicious, even brilliant manner in which he summed up the Maya in terms of their architecture was fully impressive. It must be understood that he had nothing, or next to nothing, to draw upon other than his own experience. The public, avid then as now for the sensational, had been fed on gibberish about the wandering tribes and floating Egyptians who were supposed to have peopled the ancient American world. Catherwood found Maya architecture entirely dissimilar to the Egyptian, or to anything else in the Old World; his conviction, contrary to most who were then writing on the subject, was that the Maya architecture was not of immemorial antiquity. "I do not think," he said specifically of Uxmal, "we should be safe in ascribing to any of the monuments a greater age than from eight hundred to a thousand years. . ." It was a remarkable deduction, since the Maya date-glyphs had not then been deciphered. Catherwood placed Uxmal's buildings at about 1044 A.D. The glyphs say that it was built between 987-1007 A.D.

Catherwood's conclusions about the Maya ruins anticipated many of the subsequent deductions. He insisted that they were not "the work of unknown races; but that, as we now see them, they were occupied and possibly erected by the same Indian tribes [Maya] in possession of the country at the time of the Spanish conquest — that they are the production of an indigenous school of art, adapted to the natural circumstances of the country." Finally he maintained that "they present but very slight and accidental analogies with the works of any people or country in the Old World."

The remainder of Catherwood's life was an anticlimax. Stephens had helped form the Panama Railway Company and had gone off to Panama to push it through and to acquire, among other things, the disease that would shortly kill him. Frederick Catherwood, civil engineer (he now dropped the "archt."), set off for British Guiana to build South America's first railway. One gathers from the official reports that the trip did neither him nor the rail line much good. All too often there appears in the official diary:

". . . there was considerable disagreement with Mr. Catherwood." To provide laborers Catherwood had to import negroes from Jamaica. At this the colonists complained of the abuse of their women by the migratory workers, and Catherwood had to arrange for other ladies to be available along the route of the railway. In May, 1849 — bogged down in flies, floods, and floozies — he resigned or, as the official report had it, "he was relieved for reasons of economy."

In the autumn of 1849, Catherwood was approached by Stephens's Panama Railway Company, perhaps to take over the "works" in the Isthmus, while Stephens himself went to Bogotá to straighten out a contract with the Colombian government. Catherwood was willing, but the amount of money was a problem, "as it is absolutely necessary that I should be doing something for my children who are growing up around me. My boy, who is as tall as myself, is a good classical scholar and arithmetician, so much so that I intend to bring him up as an engineer." Meantime another idea had bitten him: California. "If I were to go out to Panama it would be with the view, after my year of service had expired, to try my fortune at San Francisco. . ." That was precisely what he did.

By 1851 he was established at Benicia, "The Queen City of the Bay," then only a settlement of straggling huts. There was a scheme afoot to make Benicia the principal port in the Bay region, and to wean away the shipping from nearby San Francisco by building a railway from Marysville to Benicia, cornering the major share of California land — and commerce.

As soon as the principal merchants in San Francisco learned of the scheme, the "war of ports" began, and by that time Frederick Catherwood was very much a part of it. "I am very actively employed here engineering for the P.M.S.S. Co. [Panama Mail Steam-Ship Company]." Later he was an engineer for the Marysville-Benicia Railroad Company. "I am very pleased with my position at present. . . and have become much attached to California," so much so that he even urged Stephens to come out and enter California politics. "Why don't you become a candidate for the U.S. Senate. . . it is not too late and you would have an excellent chance of success. . ."

In 1852 Catherwood was again in England, presumably to settle his affairs and return to California since he had, contrary to his original intention to have nothing to do with the "diggings," acquired shares in the Comstock Mine. Before leaving he learned that his old friend Stephens had died in New York City, and so he arranged a new edition of Stephens's *Incidents of Travel in Central America* as a sort of memorial. As it happened, this was to be his own memorial as well.

The S.S. *Arctic* sailed from Liverpool on the twentieth of September, 1854. Many New Yorkers were aboard: there were Drews, Comstocks, Fabricottis, Howlands, Lockmiranets, Ravenscrofts, and a sprinkling of aristocracy, the most notable representative being the Duc de Gramont, returning to his post in Washington with his family. On the seventh day out of Liverpool, the sea was obscured by a thick fog blanket and at noontime, just as it began to lift, the *Arctic* collided with the S.S. *Vesta*. There were only enough lifeboats for fifty people. After frantic efforts to make rafts out of barrels and available timber, the S.S. *Arctic* went down with nearly all its three hundred passengers.

Two weeks elapsed before New Yorkers became aware of the disaster, but then the boldest type swept all else from the front pages of the city's newspapers: "THE LOSS OF THE ARTIC... THRILLING ACCOUNT BY THE CAPTAIN... SERMONS ON THE DISASTER..." The Stock Exchange closed; banks stopped their business; flags throughout the city were at half-mast. The captain of the Artic made his first statement from Quebec, where he had been brought after his rescue. It was addressed to E. K. Collins, president of the line: "Dear Sir: It becomes my painful duty to inform you of the total loss of the S.S. *Arctic,* under my command, with your wife, daughter and son..."

Then followed, day by day, name after name of the missing passengers. For two weeks the editors barred everything from the first page but details of the tragedy. One by one the survivors told of the last acts of those who had perished, and later the newspapers printed long obituaries on each of the victims, all, that is, except for the friend of Keats, Severn, Shelley, of Prescott and Bancroft; not a word of the companion of Bonomi, Robert Hay, and Wilkinson; the pioneer of Egyptology, the panoramist of

Leicester Square, the New York architect, the co-discoverer of the Maya culture, the builder of South America's first railroad. His death was to be as obscure as much of his life. Only after many days had passed did the New York *Herald,* almost as an afterthought, print the single line:

"Mr. Catherwood, also, is missing."

Bibliography of Frederick Catherwood

Views of Ancient Monuments in Central America, Chiapas, and Yucatán. London and New York, 1844.

Account of the Punico-Libyan Monument at Dougga and the Remains of an Ancient Structure at Bless, near the Site of Ancient Carthage. Transactions of the American Ethnological Society, New York, 1845, vol.I; pp. 477-91; seven figures in the text.

Incidents of Travel in Central America. Edited by F. Catherwood. Arthur Hall, Virtue & Co., London, 1854.

With Robert Burford:

Description of a View of the City of Jerusalem. . . Painted from Drawings. . . by F. Catherwood. London, 1835.

Description of a View of the Ruins of the Temple of Baalbek. . . Painted. . . from Drawings. . . by F. Catherwood. London, 1844.

Description of a View of the Great Temple of Karnak and the Surrounding City of Thebes. . . Painted by R. Burford from Drawings by Mr. F. Catherwood, London, 1839.

A Selected Bibliography of Victor Wolfgang von Hagen

CATHERWOODIANA

F. Catherwood, Architect Explorer of Two Worlds, by Victor Wolfgang von Hagen. Barre Publishers, Barre, Mass. 1968.

Maya Explorer; the Life of John Lloyd Stephens. University of Oklahoma Press, Norman, Okla. 1947. 5th edition, 1967.

Frederick Catherwood Archt. Introduction by Aldous Huxley. Oxford University Press, New York and London, 1950.

Incidents of Travel in Yucatán, by John Lloyd Stephens. Edited with an introduction by Victor W. von Hagen. University of Oklahoma Press, Norman, Okla., 1962. 2 vols.

Incidents of Travel in Arabia Petraea, by John Lloyd Stephens. Edited with an introduction and notes by Victor W. von Hagen. University of Oklahoma Press, Norman, Okla. Scheduled for 1968.

Hagen, Victor Wolfgang von: *Jungle in the Clouds,* London, 1940; *The Aztec and Maya Papermakers,* New York, 1943; F. Catherwood Archt., Bulletin of the New York Historical Society, January 1946; *How the Lost Cities of Mayas were Rediscovered,* Travel Magazine, April 1946; *Mr. Catherwood Also Is Missing,* Natural History Magazine, March 1947; *Mr. Catherwood's Panorama,* Magazine of Art, April 1947; *Maya Explorer, John Lloyd Stephens and the Lost Cities of Central America and Yucatán,* Norman, Okla.,1947; *Frederick Catherwood Archt.,* introduction by Aldous Huxley, Oxford University Press, New York and London, 1950; *Artist of a Buried World,* American Heritage, June 1961, vol. xii No. 4; *Incidents of Travel in Yucatán by John L. Stephens,* 2 vols., introduction and noted by Victor von Hagen, University of Oklahoma Press, Norman, Okla., 1963; *The Maya Explorers,* a dual biography of Stephens and Catherwood (in German), Paul Zsolnay Verlag, Wien 1968; *Incidents of Travel in Arabia Petraea,* by John L. Stephens, introduction, life, and notes by Victor W. von Hagen, University of Oklahoma, Press, Norman, Okla., 1968.

GENERAL

The Roads That Led to Rome, World Pub. Co., 1967.

The Desert Kingdoms of Perú. New York Graphic Society, Greenwich, Conn., 1965.

The Ancient Sun Kingdoms of the Americas. World Publishing Company, New York and Cleveland, 1961.

The Incas of Pedro de Cieza de León. Edited with an introduction by Victor W. von Hagen. University of Oklahoma Press, Norman Okla., 1959.

Highway of the Sun. Duell, Sloan & Pearce, New York, 1955.

The Aztec and Maya Papermakers. Introduction by Dard Hunter. J.J. Augustin, New York, 1943. (Limited to 220 copies.)

The Encantadas, or Enchanted Isles, by Herman Melville. With an introduction, critical epilogue, and bibliographical notes by Victor W. von Hagen. Grabhorn Press, San Francisco, 1940. (Limited to 750 copies)

General Bibliography

Arundale, Francis: *Illustrations of Jerusalem and Mount Sinai,* Including the Most Interesting Sites between Grand Cairo and Beyrout. London, 1837.

Bapst, G.: *Essai sur l' histoire des panoramas et des dioramas.* Paris 1891.

Belzoni, Giovanni: *Narrative of Operations and Recent Discoveries.* London, 1821.

Blomfield, Reginald: *Architectural Drawings and Draughtsmen.* London, 1912.

Dictionary of Architecture, The, 3 vols. London, 1852-93.

Fergusson, James: *History of Architecture in All Countries,* 2 vols. London, 1874.

Finden, William: *Landscape Illustrations of the Bible,* 2 vols. London, 1836.

Fox, Henry Edward: *Journal.* Edited by the Earl of Ilchester. London, 1923.

Graves, Algernon: *The Royal Academy of Arts*: A Complete Dictionary of Contributors and their Work from Its Foundation in 1769 to 1904, 8 vols. London, 1905-6.

Halle, Louis J., Jr.: *River of Ruins*. New York, 1941.

Halls, J.J.: *Life and Correspondence of Henry Salt*, 2 vols. London, 1834.

Hay, Robert: *Illustrations of Cairo*, London, 1840.

Hilmy, Ibrahim: *The Literature of Egypt and the Soudan from the Earliest Times to the Year 1885 Inclusive*: A Bibliography, London, 1886.

Hoskins, George Alexander: *A Visit to the Great Oasis of the Libyan Desert*. London, 1837.

Lane-Poole, Stanley: *Life of Edward William Lane*. London, 1877.

Newberry, Percy C.: *Topographical Notes on Western Thebes*. Annales du services des antiquitiés de L'Égypt, Paris, 1906, tome VII.

Porter, Bertha, and Moss, Rosalind: *Topographical Bibliography of Ancient Egyptian Hieroglyphic Texts, Reliefs and Paintings*, 2 vols. Oxford, 1929.

Redgrave, Samuel: *A Dictionary of Artists of the English School*. London, 1878.

Rees, Thomas:*Reminiscences of Literary London*, 1799-1853. London 1896.

Rollins, Hyder E.: *The Keats Circle...* (1806-1878), 2 vols. Cambridge, 1948.

Sabin, Joseph: *Bibliotheca Americana*, 29 vols. New York, 1868-1937. New York, 1868-1937.

Sandby, William: *History of the Royal Academy*, London, 1862.

Thieme-Becker: *Allgemeines Lexikon der Bildenden Kunstler*. Leipzig, 1907.

Wilkinson, Sir John G.: *Thebes and Egypt*. London 1927.

Wood and Dakins: *Baalbek*. London,1757.